ROOTED & GROUNDED

A GUIDE TO MARITAL WHOLENESS

Author: Nyenye Jordan

Rooted and Grounded

A Guide to Marital Wholeness

Copyright @2023 Nyenye Jordan

ISBN: 9798871343678

December 2023

All Scripture quotations are taken for the King James Version of the Bible

All rights reserved. It is not legal to reproduce, duplicate, or transmit any part of this document in either electronic means or printed format. Recording of this publication is strictly prohibited.

This book is dedicated to: My Husband, My Mom, & My Children

Thank each of you for allowing me to grow and complete this portion of my Purpose.

It is dedicated to every marriage that the enemy thought that he had broken. It is dedicated to every woman who is or was at their wits end and had nowhere else to turn. It is dedicated to every husband that surrendered to God so that his marriage can be healed and whole. This is a testament to the goodness of God, His Grace and Mercy.

As you embark on this journey into creating a healthy, whole relationship, please allow God to have His Way. Allow the Holy Spirit to minister to you and your spouse. Shut out the outside distractions. That includes the friends, the naysayers, the negative Nancy's, and whoever else is speaking against your relationship. You stop negatively speaking about your marriage. **Speak the Word only!! Ok I'm about to take a text!! I better save it for the book.**

BE BLESSED, I'M ROOTING FOR YOU,

Love,

Coach Nyenye J

TABLE OF CONTENTS

Introduction..1-4

Chapter 1: The Anantomy of Your Marriage......6-11

Chapter 2: Let's Talk about IT 12-17

Chapter Three: Partnership ,,,,,,,,,,,,,,,,,,,,,,,,,,,18-26

Chapter Four: Show Me the Money!!! 27-33

Chapter Five: Bag Lady 34-46

 Chapter Six CHANGE..........................47-74

Chapter Seven: The Evolution.................75-79

Chapter Eight: Let's talk About Sex..........80-90

Chapter 9: In-Laws, & MORE................91-97

Note from the Author.............................98

Acknowledgements..........................99-102

About the Author...............................103

v

Introduction

Thank you for purchasing this book. I am excited to embark on this journey with you.

This book is about creating the marriage/relationship that you desire using Biblical Principles. A marriage filled with not only what you desire but that is filled with God desires for you. This is a roadmap for your relationship. A guide that is based on Christian principles and protocols. I tried to write this book and leave God out. You know how we sometimes don't want to push God on people, but the Spirit of God spoke to me, and I am speaking to you. We cannot do it without God. He is the head of the church and the head of our marriage.

You are at a crossroad. The enemy has used you against your marriage. The very thing that you prayed for has become a burden. The one person that you made a covenant agreement with has now become public enemy number one. This is not what you signed up for, is it? I want you to know that you are not alone. Since the conception of marriage, the enemy has used spouse against spouse in an effort to dismantle the institution of marriage. Sometimes the enemy is us. The person that we have allowed ourselves to become.

But I want you to remember that love that made you want to get married. I want you to remember the joy in your heart.

This book explores the trials and tribulations of marriage and how to face them using God's Word. I will walk you through different scenarios and give you guidance on how to react or not react. I will walk you through effective communication, how to create a partnership, financial literacy in marriage and so much more. By the end of this book, you will have realized that you are both on the same team, with the same goal in mind – happily ever after. (yes, you can have that happily ever after, it is not a fairy tale) I invite you to laugh, cry, apologize, embrace, and all the things, so that you create the marriage that you desire. I have been where you are and these principles along with Christian Coaching, have healed my marriage. My husband and I were at a Crossroad in our life. We did not even want to be at the same house with each other, pulling in the driveway and sitting, EXPECTING the next argument, looking for a way out. Just like you, God did not release us from our marriage, but he gave us the tools to fix what was broken. Are you ready to fix wat is broken? Are you ready to get your TEAM back? Are you ready to be IN LOVE again?

You are reading the right book at the right time!!!! This is your season to take back what the devil attempted to take from you!! Let's get it started!! Start reading today and begin your journey into a HEALTHY AND WHOLE MARRIAGE!!!

Goals as I read this book:

1. _____
   _____
   _____
   _____
   _____
   _____

2. _____
   _____
   _____
   _____
   _____
   _____

3. _____
   _____
   _____
   _____
   _____
   _____

4. _____
   _____
   _____

5.

6.

7.

8.

CHAPTER 1: The Anatomy of Your Marriage

It begins with a seed.

When I look back, and think about why I got married, I realize that it began with a seed. The seed of love, the desire for companionship and the idea that two are better than one. Those ideas were planted in my mind as a child. I saw my mother and father as a married couple, creating a life together. My father would look at my mother with eyes that showed so many different emotions. The one that I am most fond of is when he looked at her and loved her with his eyes. He looked at her as if she was the only woman in the world. As I observed their relationship the seed was planted in me. I began to desire to be married. I longed to have a man look at me in that way. I wanted to be loved the way my mother had been loved. What I realized later, after I was married, is that I really needed to be loved like God loves.

Now that is not to say that their marriage was perfect because no marriage is perfect. The fact of the matter is that I saw what a husband "looked-like". Now that the seed was planted in my heart and my mind, I had to make sure that the seed was surrounded by good soil. That is where my commitment to follow Christ was strengthened. I knew that we as people falter, but I know that God was not like man. I recognized that if I continued to nourish my relationship with God, I would be able to create a marriage that was nourished as well. What is unfortunate, and part of the reason that I am writing this book is that I went about it all wrong. I forgot about the need for good soil, I even forgot that I was a good seed. I allowed my flesh and people to dictate and influence how I navigated in my marriage. At one point I even put my beliefs to the side. I was going to do things my way, and believe me, I reaped my results.

As we go on, I want you to imagine that your marriage is a tree. By the end of this book, you will be planted by the rivers of water (Jeremiah 17:7-8). Now you may feel like your tree has been uprooted, or even rotten at the core, BUT just take this journey and allow God to revive, restore and renew what was thought to be dead. The tree has roots that are deeply planted in the soil. Shooting out of the ground is the trunk of the tree. On the tree are many branches, the branches have many leaves. Sometimes we have to get some of the roots and replant them in a different area. That may mean moving to another area, getting a different job, or even severing some relationships. Whatever God leads you to do, my prayer is that you are obedient to His instructions. As we go further, I will show you how your tree is going to be renewed and nourished.

As a wife I want you to understand your purpose in marriage. We as women are a help meet for our husbands. We are there to help them fulfill the purpose that God has planted in them. That is not to say that your purpose will not be fulfilled. Together you are a team, designed by God, for a purpose. Together you can create a legacy of love, an example that gives people a glimpse of how much Christ loves the church, his bride. This is much deeper than two people having a crush on each other. This is a ministry. God is the head of your union and even when one of you are off task, the other is there to intercede and petition God.

Genesis 2:18

"And the Lord God said, It is not good that man should be alone; I will make him an help meet for him.

The Hebrew word for help meet is ezer kenegdo. The word ezer translates to help, but it does not mean the way that we typically view help. It is not as a servant or maid, but as a rescuer. The ezer is seen as a person who rescues her husband. Doesn't that change your perspective of who you are as a wife? I hope it empowers you and that you realize that you have been united with your husband because you are the answer to his prayers. Whether he realizes it or not. The term ezer describes strength. Ezer is used 21 times in the Old

Testament, always describing a person with the capacity allowing one to help, protect, or aid. In most cases Ezer describes the way God offered help to rescue mankind.

Kenegdo means "corresponding to" or opposite to". It describes two things that are next to each other and complement each other but are different from each other. Putting these two terms together gives us the idea that God created Eve in counterpart to Adam, with the power to rescue and serve. This is the acknowledgement of our strength as women.

I often tell women that the man is the head, but we are the neck. We have the God given capability to help control the course of our marriage. We can do so in such a way that your husband retains his position as the head. This is not about titles; it is about purpose. When you got married it was not just to get his last name, it was to be united with him. To have a constant companion, a friend, a confidante, a prayer partner, and the list goes on. What many women do not recognize is that our husbands, the head of our homes, is not perfect. I know many of you said, "He is perfect for me." I will agree with that but sooner or later his flaws and your flaws will start to show up in your marriage if they haven't already. When that happens, you will need the tools to rescue him, to save the marriage, to restore the love. This is not the time to run away. This is the time to go to war for your marriage. Your marriage is a covenant agreement that you did not come into lightly. Your marriage is a testament of God's goodness and mercy. It will tell of story. It is part of your legacy. There were vows and a declaration of love that created a bond that is not meant to be easily broken. You made that vow before God. Are you ready to take your position of purpose seriously? Are you dedicated to remaining committed to the man you married? Marriage is a ministry.

Some of you may be saying that you are more than a wife. To that I say, "YES, you are." At the same time the position of wife is a ministry that God ordained. It is special to Him. It is reflective of His relationship with the church. It is a representation of His undying love for us, His children. Do not despise what you were created for. The world will try to belittle the title, Wife. God allowed you to be a wife because you desired it. You are a blessing to your husband. He blesses your husband through his treatment of you. Embrace your role as a wife. Allow God through the words of this book to renew and restore your love, respect, trust, and desire for your husband and your marriage.

To fulfill your purpose in your marriage you must petition God and allow yourself to be led by the Holy Spirit.

The Holy Spirit is here as leader and a guide, He is also a comforter. Those nights when things are not going as planned in your marriage and feel as though as hope is gone, allow the Holy Spirit to comfort you. The storm will not last always, but we delay the promise when we act out of emotions and ignore the guidance of the Holy Spirit.

Lord, we thank you for using this book to restore marriages, renew relationships, and teach us how to draw closer to You, in the name of Jesus. Amen

Chapter Two: Let's Talk about IT
Effective Communication

Communication is the lifeline of any relationship.

Elizabeth Bourgeret

I want to start this chapter with the definition of the word, Communication.

Communication: the imparting or exchanging of information or news.

A means of sending or receiving information.

The successful conveying or sharing of ideas and feelings.

Social contact.

Now as we go further, we will explore each of these definitions. When we communicate, we share information with each other. We should be doing it in such a manner that the person on the receiving end is eager to listen and receive the information, whether it is good or bad news. Communication does not just begin with the words that come from our mouths. It begins with the tone of our voice, the expressions on our face and the INTENT OF OUR HEART.

If you would be honest sometimes, we begin conversations with the intent to hurt the person that we are talking to. We want to add shock value because we think that it will make our mate listen more effectively or do what we want them to do. That is using intimidation and manipulation. I promise you that those are not the tactics that you should use if you desire a healthy, whole relationship. Think about it, would you want someone to use those tactics on you? (And as ye would that men should do to you, do ye also to them likewise. Luke 6:31) so maybe you are asking, how should I communicate, especially when I am angry or feel betrayed? I am glad you asked. You should communicate in love and out of a pure heart. Allow God to give you the words to say and how to deliver them. I have learned in my marriage that some issues I do not even take to my husband. I offer them to God in prayer and I leave them there. I know that may seem crazy, but it does work. The key is to leave it there.

Honest Communication

More times than not, we are not honest with each other. We do not want to hurt our partner's feelings. The problem with that is that in the end you both are hurt. There is a way to be honest and be kind at the same time. The enemy wants us, especially in marriage, to feel like the more we cut into our spouse the more they get our point. If we hurt them, they will see that we really mean business and that is not true. You do not have to be cruel to make our point. The Bible tells us that we get more from honey than we do with vinegar. (Proverbs 16:24 Pleasant words are a honeycomb, sweet to the soul and healing to the bones.) In a time of disagreement do you believe that you can lift a person up? Communication is not about tearing down although there may be a period of peeling off layers. The result should always be growth and healing. This is when we need to think about the motive of our conversation. Are you purposely being mean? Are you aiming to hurt his feelings?

Why are you saying the things that you are saying? Anger is a dangerous emotion. People say and do things out of anger that they would not necessarily do if they weren't angry. Remember that you cannot take words back once they come out of your mouth. Therefore, it is important that we choose them wisely. (Proverbs 21:23) We have heard that "hurt people, hurt people" and that is true. If you are hurt, you will continue to hurt people. Especially those that are closest to you. Your spouse is not the enemy !!! This is the person that you are creating a partnership with. I think we go into arguments with the mindset that we are in a battle and there must be a defined winner. This is so far from the truth. This is a difference of opinion, not war. You are a both are on the same team.

Effective Communication is the process of exchanging ideas, thoughts, opinions, knowledge, and data so that the message is received and understood with clarity and purpose. This means that when we communicate/talk to each other it should be for a clear and concise purpose. This speaks to the motives of your words. To effectively communicate the atmosphere must be conducive, meaning it must be a non-hostile environment. That is why many times we must wait until we have cooled off to talk to each other, and that is okay. It is preferred. Who really listens to someone when they are barking at us? So, we need to be calm and ready to listen, as well as tell our side of the issue. This may mean that you need a moment of silence prior to having that needed conversation. It may mean that you need to take a few deep breaths. Ask God to give you a heart and mind to speak objectively, to express yourself in a kind manner. Pray that God will allow you to hear as well as be heard. Ask God to fix your heart and his heart before the discussion begins. Many times, my husband and I pray prior to having the hard discussions.

Listening is an art of its own. You do not truly hear what a person is saying when you are interrupting them and trying eagerly to get your turn to talk. When you are listening, you take in their words without biases or negative body language. Listen with the intention to understand what they are saying. Too many times we listen with the desire to speak our piece/peace. (no pun intended.) That is a disservice to your partnership. We all want others to understand our point of view. The Bible says that we should treat others the way that we desire to be treated. Do you want your partner to listen to you without biases or interruption? We expect our bosses/supervisors to listen to our needs/desires, right? So, how is it that we do not understand the importance of listening to our PARTNER? The one that we have made a covenant agreement with …make it make sense. Sis, the enemy does not want your marriage to work so he doesn't want you to be a good listener. Listening also helps you know what to pray for. It also leads to questioning what you can do better? How can you contribute so that there is a better outcome? A partner who feels that they have been truly heard tends to listen better and respond to the needs of their partner. Sis, it is time to tune up your listening skills. Watch your marriage blossom.

I find that is good practice to write things down. Jotting down the key points helps you to address each one. Also, when you are listening you are attempting to understand their perspective. Ask yourself questions like:

- How would that make me feel?

- How could I have handled the situation better?
- What was my intent at that time ?
- Was I clear about my intention/actions ?

As you make those mental assessments you will find that there are more effective ways to handle your issues and that it is important to hear what is being said than to rush to get your turn. Once your partner has voiced their opinion, go back to your outlined points, and address them individually. Remain calm, even if there is a point that you strongly disagree with. Keep your cool. Remember this is the person that you love and desire to spend your life with. They are not the enemy. You both are on the SAME TEAM. Even if we disagree, we must be respectable and open to each other. That leads us to the next topic of discussion, Creating a Partnership.

Chapter Three
Partnership: A Covenant Agreement

What does partnership mean…

The state of being a partner or partners. So, let's break that down, and look at what the word partner means.

Partner – either of a pair of people engaged together in the same activity. Individuals with interest and investments in a business or enterprise, among whom expenses, profits and losses are shared.

While we are looking up words, let us we what marriage is defined as.

Marriage - a legally or formally recognized union of two people as partners in a relationship.

Now my prayer is that you invited God to the relationship before the wedding plans began. That is where many of us mess up. We get into relationships based on outward appearance, words of flattery, or sexual appeal. Now is the time to invite God into your marriage/relationship. The marriage should be composed of three, God, the Man, and the Woman. Those should be the key components to every marriage and relationship. Where is Christ in your union? Did you invite Christ to the ceremony? Did you seek the guidance of the Holy Spirit as you made plans, picked your dress, etc.? If you did not invite God to be the head of your union, let's invite Him now.

Prayer:

Heavenly Father,

We/I invite you to come into our union. As every plan is made, we/I invite you to be our lead and guide. We ask you to lead us as we prepare to become one. Our prayer is that even as we go through trials and tribulations that we will look to you together for guidance. Speak to our spirits collectively so that we will be on one accord. Give us the wisdom to be open and honest with each other without offense. We thank you in advance for your guidance. Remind us when we step out of alignment with Your Word and with each other so that we can realign and get back on the right path. We do not want to do anything without you and your approval. We thank you for being a lamp unto our feet and a light unto our paths. Show us how to love each other as you have loved us. In Jesus Name, Amen

Things are really coming together now. I find that it is easier to navigate a thing when we are clear about the thing. Makes sense, right? So, you have created a partnership that has been labeled by the world as Marriage. It usually consists of a ceremony. You invite people that care about you and your mate to the ceremony. They celebrate, congratulate, and give you their blessings on your wedding day. It is acknowledged by the government as a formal union, consensual by the two parties. It is usually an awesome day… with maybe a few snags, lol. All in all, it is the day where you partner with the person that you love to spend the rest of your life with. Congratulations.

Now this is where the rubber meets that road. You are now forging a life together. After the ceremony and all the partying, what is next? Will the honeymoon phase last forever? Will the dating continue? Will the two really become one? Is the fairytale just beginning or will it end abruptly? These are some of the questions that many of us have after the wedding is over. Now we must live in the real world and face life together. Two imperfect people coming together to create a life together. Will we be successful, or will we fail?

I want to encourage you to look at this new life using biblical principles. It is easy to get caught up in what your Madea, Aunt or BFF did, but remember this marriage is between God, You and Your Spouse. You do not have to repeat the mistakes of the past. Nor do you have to duplicate the mistakes of others. You can be led by the Holy Spirit every step of the way. Let us go to the scriptures.

Ephesians 5:22-27

> 22 Wives submit to your own husband, as to the Lord. 23 For the husband is the head of the wife, as also Christ is head of the church; and He is Savior of the body, 24 Therefore just as the church is subject to Christ, so let the wives be to their own husbands in everything.

Now let's break the scripture down. (Feel free to read it in other translations such as the Amplified and New Living Translation) This is saying we as wives should be willing to submit (accept or yield to the authority of) as he is following the Lord. Now let me put a few disclaimers here. Wives you know whether your husband was saved prior to your wedding ceremony. So do not use this scripture as a basis to be disrespectful after marriage. I hear women say, "Well he does not submit to God, so I do not have to submit to him." As long as he is leading in a respectable way that lines up with the will of God submit to his leadership. Many men receive love through trust and respect, so if you desire your marriage to be healthy and whole, maintain a level of trust and respect for your husband, even when things are not going as planned. This passage of scripture tells us clearly that God intended for the husband to be the head of the marriage partnership. Does that mean that he makes all the decisions? Absolutely not. This book is to empower women in their marriage so I will not get into all of the duties of a husband, but I will say that we must remember that this is a partnership. We are on the same team. That being said, we must support each other and effectively communicate with each other about everything.

This is where your prayer life really comes into play. I tell women that it is necessary to be proactive in your marriage and not reactive. Many times, we react after the enemy has reared his ugly head when we should have been praying over our husbands before the issues presented themselves. Pray that you can submit to your husband. Pray that he becomes a leader that is worthy of leading. Pray that God create the leader that He desires your husband to be. Remember we may want one thing, but God knows what is best. We always want God's will to be done in our lives. He knows what is best for us. He has plans to prosper us. (Jeremiah 29:11) As a team we should desire to prosper together. We are building. As women we have been given the ability to multiple and create. As God and our husbands sow into us, we create MORE. We allow for expansion in our homes, our hearts, and our lives. Also remember that you are a rescuer. (ezer kenegdo) In prayer you recuse your husband from the attacks of the enemy. You complement him. There may be some things that you do not see eye to eye on but by coming together and compromising you can create a heck of a legacy. Remember that the enemy comes to kill, steal, and destroy but Christ has come that you may have life more abundantly.

Defeat the enemy daily so that your marriage will reflect that abundant life. (John 10:10)

"But he's not leading."

What do you do when your husband is simply not leading? I know that many of us have situations where your husband, the proclaimed head, is not leading like you think he should be or even how the Bible says that he should be leading. I want you to know that this is another trick of the enemy. The enemy attacks the men because they have been declared by God as leaders. He does not want them to be leaders in the home, in the church, or in the community. He wants them to fail because if they fail there is a higher probability that the family as a whole will fail. So, know that this is bigger than you and your partner. When it comes to your specific situation, I suggest that you begin with praying to the Father:

Heavenly Father,

I want to thank you for my husband, _____. I love the way he _____. _____. _____ and _____. Here lately we have not been on one accord, and I am praying that You lead us and guide us so that we align ourselves and our marriage to the Word of God. The Word says that _____(insert your husband's name) is the head of the household. I desire to submit to _____ but he is not submitting to you currently. I pray that you re-align his heart and his mind to do your will and lead this household. Lord, please keep me in all thy ways so that I remain the wife that you have instructed me to be. Allow me to love in spite of our current marital condition. Keep my heart and motives pure. Lord, help me to continue to pray for him and show him love. Let me hear clearly from You. Thank You Jesus for hearing and answering my prayer. In Jesus name, Amen

The next order of business is to affirm what you desire by speaking it and journaling. Go to scripture in the Bible that describe the duty of a husband. Here are a few:

Scripture Reference:

1. Ecclesiastes 9:9
2. Colossians 3:19
3. Ephesians 5:25, 5:28
4. 1 Peter 3:7

Meditate on these scriptures, not to call your husband out on all of his transgressions or offensives but, use them as a guide in your prayers for him and your marriage. Remember we are always praying God's Will for our lives and our marriage.

Our heart can at times be far from God, it can be selfish, angry, disappointed, etc., and in those times, we may not pray the Will of God, so we must keep the scriptures near so that we pray the right prayers with the right motive.

The next thing that we you must do is LISTEN to the voice of God. Once again, your prayer was not only for your husband but for you to hear from God for further instruction. So now is the time to carve out time in your schedule to just sit in the presence of God and listen for his instruction. Do not be hasty and harsh in your actions. So many times, I was quick to react to situations on my marriage. I lived to regret those hasty actions. I did not listen to God when he told me to hold up and hold out. I told people things that should have been just between God, me & my husband. I said words that were against our marriage and that essentially caused destructive consequences for my marriage. I do not want you to have to experience that type of hurt and pain. It is nothing like looking your spouse in the face and realizing that you have added to their pain and hurt. Listen to the voice of God and do what he tells you to do, when He tells you to do it. A delay in obedience is disobedience. If you truly want God to restore and renew your husband and your marriage, be obedient to God above all else.

Chapter Four
Show me the Money!! Financial Literacy in Marriage

Let me begin with this disclaimer: I am NOT a financial advisor. I am sharing my experiences of how bad financial practices affected my marriage.

Now that that is out of the way, let's get into it !!! Money is a motivator. Many people do strange things for money. Some people get married simply because their partner has money. Money can also be a branch of discord within a marriage. It really isn't the money that is the culprit, but it is usually the mismanagement, dishonesty, and manipulation that is attached to the money that is the real culprit. It is my suggestion that you and your partner get financial counseling from an actual financial advisor PRIOR to marriage if you both are not on the same page before getting married. There should be discussions about your finances during your marriage counseling sessions. You do not want to go into a marriage with unrealistic expectations about money and finances.

First things first, PUT ALL THE CARDS ON THE TABLE. I encourage both of you to be open and honest about your finances. You need to reveal the good, the bad and the ugly prior to tying the knot. In the previous chapter we discussed the husband being the head of the household. Just because he is the head of the household does not mean that he is the expert on everything in the marriage. Your husband may not be the best money manager and that is okay. The key is allowing whoever is the expert to be over that aspect of the marriage. In my case my husband is a good money manager, he believes in paying for things on time and in full. I believe in paying on things and having the bulk of the money at my disposal. (I am doing better at this) I learned to let my husband lead except for when it came to getting cars. My husband has been an impulse buyer when it comes to cars. He is never really satisfied. So, we have to go into deep prayer when we are looking to get a new vehicle. We realize then and go into with God's guidance. You need to recognize your strengths and weaknesses within your finances and act accordingly. If neither of you are good when it comes to finances, seek the help of a professional. Do not let pride get in the way of having financial stability.

When you lay down all the cards on the table that means disclosing all financial information to each other. Many of you just clutched your proverbial pearls. I know that many women have been taught to leave some money to that side that your husband does not know about. Many of you have been taught to maintain separate bank accounts, additional life insurance, etc. I totally understand the reasoning behind these perspectives. I also want to bring it to let you know that that is going into the marriage with secrets. You must decide if these secrets are worth keeping. I do not suggest keeping secrets at all. The truth is always better than a lie and, in my opinion, keeping secrets (withholding information) is lying. If it comes out that your husband has another account later in your marriage, how will you honestly feel about it? What if he has an additional insurance policy that has a past lover as a beneficiary?

I can see you know saying but, "That is not the same." Or "I had this money before we started our relationship/" Does that mean that you must keep it a secret? Do you want a marriage where you give him your body but not share your money? Even if you do not put his name on the account, don't you think that he should at least be aware that the account exists?

It truly amazes me that so many people are willing to share their bodies and be intimate with each other but keep secrets and separate accounts when it comes to money. That shows where our hearts are. Do not kill the messenger but the Bible clearly states that where a person's treasure is, there is also where their heart is. (Matthew 6:21 For where your treasure is, there your heart will be also.) Decide if your heart is in "the marriage" and your desire is to navigate marriage using Godly principles or is your heart more concerned with your money? I have found that the main reason that people keep these types of financial secrets is because they are making sure that they are not left with no money IF the marriage is dissolved. That is making plans for if the marriage does not work out. If you go into a marriage making plans in the case of its demise, what are you saying about your faith in the marriage? If you change your perspective and say I am going to give this marriage all that I have because I love and believe in our union, including full disclosure of my financial status and desires, then I think that you have a better chance of financial and marital success.

The mind and the heart are the areas that the enemy wants to have full control of. If he can manipulate your thinking, then he can surely take over your heart. What I am essentially saying is that do not make money your main focus in your marriage. Do not allow the love or the pursuit of money, replace the joy of marriage and creating a life with the person that you love. Money will come and go but the opportunity to love and be loved by another person is priceless.

That does not mean that you have the license to be financially irresponsible. Money and the lack of it can cause strain on your marriage. That is why honesty is so important. So, here are some key points when dealing with finances:

1. Be honest, Full disclosure.

2. Let whoever is the best with the finances do the budget. Write it out together.

3. Remember that you are partners so make decisions together that support what is best for you both.

4. Have rules that you have agreed upon. For example, consult your partner for purchases over $500. You come together and decide what those rules and limits are.

5. If anyone other than your spouse is a beneficiary to any policy or account, please disclose that information.

6. Do not be too proud to seek professional financial support.

Scriptures on the heart and the mind:

1. Psalms 51:10

2. Colossians 3:2

3. Romans 12:2

4. Ephesians 4:23

5. Philippians 4:8

6. Proverbs 3:5

Prayer:

Lord, lead us and guide us in our finances. We do not want to miss out on quality time and making memories because of bad financial decisions. Allow us to be in alignment concerning our finances. Let us not be too proud to admit when we need help. Do not let our past perspectives cloud our vison for our financial future. Allow us to renew our minds in your Word so that we make decisions together that are for the best. Let us be open and honest about our financial concerns with one another. Let neither of us be easily offended, help us to remember that we are a team and that we are led by You. Holy Spirit be a lamp unto our feet and a light into our paths. In the name of Jesus, Amen.

Chapter 5

Bag Lady: How to get pass the Pain & Trauma (Extra Baggage)

Baggage is heavy, bulky, and hard to carry most of the time. When you are talking about personal baggage from relationships, trauma, and pain, you are talking about some heavy stuff. To many times we carry this baggage into each relationship. We carry it into our marriages. We use it against our spouses. It rests in the recesses of our mind, waiting, lurking to come out at the wrong time. It creates arguments. It stunts growth. It cripples us. So why do we hold on to it?

For many of us, we think that it keeps us safe. It's a wall that we create to keep people out. It's a trigger that we hold onto so that the alarm goes off and we do not end up in the same situation again. Yet here we are. Keeping the baggage has not eased our fears. It has not provided safety. It has increased our fear and inability to create the relationship/marriage that we desire. This is your sign to let it go. Dump all the baggage in the trash. Take your finger off the trigger and throw the gun away. It is time to build from the ground up. (*Philippians 3:13-14 but this one thing I do,* *forgetting those things which are behind, and reaching forth unto those things which are before,)*That means that we are no longer looking behind us. The past constantly wants to keep us in bondage. We start arguments with the famous words, "remember when you did ..." That garbage fuels your fears and insecurities. Now that is not to say that your feelings are not valid. Those things may have happened, but it is time to deal with them differently. It is time to look at it from a different perspective. Use whatever life lesson you learned and move on.

Maybe you are wondering what I mean by baggage. I mean the situations that keep you up at night, The things that you are scared to tell your spouse. The skeletons in your closet. Anything that keeps you from showing up in your marriage as a healthy and whole person. For many years in my marriage, I was broken. Not because of anything that had happened in the marriage but because of the things that had happened prior to the marriage. I had been through many traumatic experiences, and they had a chokehold on me. I had tried to deal with them on my own, but I was unsuccessful. I began to take my bitterness out on my husband, I was mad because he could not fix me, I thought that as a husband he would dress and heal all my wounds. What ai found is that he was not capable of healing my wounds. It was not his "job" to heal my wounds, He did have the capacity to heal my wounds, he did not even know the depths of my pain and trauma. On top of all of that he had issues of his own, I was asking him to do what God says in His Word that He would do. (Psalm 147:3 - He heals the brokenhearted and binds up their wounds.)

Baggage puts too much weight on the marriage. It distracts from what marriage is really designed for. Now that is not to say that we are going to enter marriage as perfect beings. The key to creating a healthy marriage is being able to identify the issues and addressing the issues head on. I truly suggest that couples practice marriage maintenance. For some that may be the need to meet with a Coach or Counselor once a month, for others that may mean meeting every three months, or even twice a year. Each couple must decide what is best fitted for their union. You must know that marriage counseling does not mean that you are weak or that your marriage is weak, it means that you are willing to do the work to create a healthy, whole marriage.

Baggage shows up as many things in a relationship. It may be that you have never healed from past self-confidence issues, body image issues, internal anger issues, or any number of things. These issues will show up at the most inopportune times and will manifest in an argument. Now your mate did not cause that particular issue, but the enemy will cause you to argue with them because of your hurt and pain. They are the closest person to you and so you lash out at them. They do not even understand why you are coming at them with such anger. Or maybe they have angered you in some way and it has triggered memories from a past issue. Now you have gone rogue over what looks to be a simple misunderstanding. These are the tools that the enemy uses to cause chaos and confusion into the marriage that God ordained, it begins to feel like you made a bad decision. You begin to doubt that God even wanted you to get married in the first place. This is the web of deception that many marriages fall prey to. I do not want this for your marriage. Can you see where this has happened within your marriage? Can you be honest with yourself and say that it wasn't just your spouse, but it stemmed from some "baggage" that you have not released?

There are ways that you can rid your marriage of this baggage. You can allow God to fix what is broken in your marriage by prayer and submission to His Will for your marriage. It means that you must allow Him to deal with you and transform you. So many times, I thought that all God had to do was change my husband and all the time God was saying that He wanted to change me. He changed my perspective, how I was seeing things. He reminded me of the love that I had for my husband prior to marriage, and how we had communicated so freely prior to marriage. The most important thing that he showed me was that my relationship with Him was suffering. I had made my marriage & my husband my idol. I was looking to my husband to make me happy when God wanted to be the source of my happiness and my joy. This transformation will look different for each of us but the core of it will be the same.

First, we must seek God. We must listen to what God has to say specifically about our situation. I used to look at other marriages and try to emulate what I thought was going on in their marriage. We see that very often in relationships, where people try to do what they think is working in other relationships, especially celebrity marriages. The fact of the matter is that we do not know what is really going on in these marriages. Now there is nothing wrong with admiring other marriages but know that God wants to deal with you specifically on what is needed for your marriage. Be open and honest with God. Cry out to Him. Confide in Him. When talking to God be open to admitting your faults and flaws. He knows them anyway so there is no shame in verbalizing them to Him now. So now you are entering a place where there is complete surrender. This is a good place to be in. It is ok to be vulnerable in this moment. As you conversate with God also allow time to LISTEN to what God says to you. This is your time to let go of the pride, the preconceived notions, the anger, and anything that has separated you from God and listening to His instruction.

Now this may be done by yourself or with your partner. That part does not really matter at this point. What matters is that there is a release and an acceptance of God's Will. This is the pivotal moment in your marriage. This is where the spiritual transformation begins and real change manifests from the inside out. Meditation is not only talking to God, but it is LISTENING to God. We must open our hearts and mind to hear from God for correction, direction, and reproof (expression of disapproval). Many times, we just want praise from God but as you enter this season of transformation and allowing God to remove the baggage from your marriage/relationship, you must be able to take the constructive criticism. It is not easy. We rarely want to hear anyone point out our "bad" or negative behavior, but it is necessary for true transformation.

What is the baggage that you are attempting to rid your relationship of? There are issues in our lives that we have told ourselves that we will never get rid of. For instance, infidelity is an issue in so many marriages and relationships. People feel as though if a person cheats on you then they never really loved you in the first place. I want you to know that this is not true in most cases. The issue becomes that people are so convinced in their minds that infidelity means that the person did not love them that they don't even seek a solution. But if the two people are committed to change, are committed to each other, and are committed to God they can restore their marriage. Now, let me be clear that it takes two people agreeing to get past many of these issues, but the change can begin with you. A healthy whole marriage does not look the same for each couple. So do not look at others and try to be a carbon copy of what you assume they have. You and your partner get together with God and allow him to create the strategy for your marriage. That works because God always wants what is best and what he provides always lines up with his word. This transformation takes a lot of patience and understanding from both parties involved. God knows and He cares, and He desires for your marriage to be healthy and whole.

> Are you ready to let go of the baggage?
>
> Are you ready to release all of the pain and past trauma?
>
> Are you ready to start the journey into wholeness and healing?
>
> Are you willing to allow this journey to begin with you?
>
> Have you heard the voice of God concerning your marriage?

Are you committed to keeping God the head of your marriage?

Has your mate expressed any commitment to this t transformation?

Have you looked for coaching or counseling to deal with the issues in your marriage?

Are you ready to be open and honest about the changes that are needed within yourself and your relationship?

Are you ready to go through some hard nights and days for the good of a healthy whole marriage?

Are you committed to allowing God to transform you as he transforms your marriage?

If you have said yes to most of the questions above, then I believe that you are ready and committed to starting the transformation process. Let me be the first one to say to you. "Congratulations"! It takes a lot of courage to allow God to change you from the inside out. It takes a lot of courage to go through the trauma and pain and to relive some of these moments, but I promise you that if God did it for me, He can do it for you too. I want you to know that it won't be easy but if this is God's will for your life, He will get you through it. Remember to consult Him every step of the way. I can remember days when I stood in the parking lot of my church and I said Lord if it is not your will for us to be together please, take away my love for him and I can imagine that he also petitioned God to make some changes about how he felt for me but in the end love prevailed and not just lust not just for financial reasons or any of those things but true love prevailed. Today I can say that we are friends, we are lovers, we are confidants, we are everything that God promised us that we could be for each other.

Prayer:

Lord, we thank you for allowing us to cleanse our marriage of any baggage from past trauma or pain. We thank you for allowing our marriage to be free of any pain or trauma that we created within the marriage because of disobedience, ignorance, anger, strife, etc. We humbly submit our marriage back to you. We ask you to create in us a clean heart and renew that right Spirit within us.

We stand on the truth of your Word about our marriage. Allow our marriage to be held in honor above all. Let us be patient and kind to one another. We will not be dishonorable or rude, we will always lift each other up and practice love. We will have an ear to hear each other and a heart to correct what is wrong within the marriage.

We commit to seek Godly counsel when needed and to do the work to maintain a Godly marriage. We understand that there will be good and bad days, and we know that with you as the head of our lives and our marriage we will be victorious.

In Jesus name we pray, Amen.

Scriptures to reference as you seek got to rid your marriage of "baggage":

(some of these are repeated from other sections)

1. Psalms 51:10-12
2. Romans 12:2
3. 2nd Corinthians 3:17-18
4. Jeremiah 29:12-13
5. Ephesians 4:32
6. Colossians 3:13
7. Proverbs 17:9
8. Mark 11:25-26
9. Luke 17:3-4

Notes

_____

_____

_____

Nyenye – Rooted & Grounded

Chapter Six: C.H.A.N.G.E.

C-Compromise **H**-Healing **A**-Acknowledgement

N-Necessary **G**-Grace **E**-Evolution

Life is full of changes and many of those changes are challenging. Marriages are challenging because it is the forging of two different people into one household for what is designed to be a lifetime. When you look at the parameters of traditional marriage it can be overwhelming to imagine. You mean to say that that I am committing to one person for the rest of my life? This is where perspective really matters. It is all in how you look at it. Then there is that person that says, "Nothing matters but Love, we can get through anything." Each one of those statements focuses on an extreme view of marriage. There is so much more to consider in between those statements. That is where marriage and the mindset concerning your marriage transforms. When I first entered my marriage, I was imagining the white picket fence, 2.5 kids, and a goldfish (I didn't want a dog). I did not take into consideration the arguments, differences of opinion, baby mama's, stepchildren, in laws, and the part that they would play in our marriage. (We will address that specifically in the next chapter) Once these issues began to influence our marriage, I knew that I would have to embrace **C.H.A.N.G.E. (Some have more than one application)**

Compromise

:settle a dispute by mutual concession.

This is the definition that we associate with the word compromise - accept standards that are lower than is desirable. But that is not what happens when you compromise with your mate.

Compromise does not mean that you must accept standards that are low, the terms of your agreement may not be what you first envisioned but that too can change. All relationships require some level of compromise from time to time. Remember the two have become one. That means that for you both to live peacefully there will be times when you get your way and other times when he gets his way. The goal is to both be satisfied and happy. That means that you need to think of their needs as much as you think of your own. It is hard to do this (I want to say that it is impossible) without God leading you. Mutual concession is the key.

Commitment – the state or quality of being committed to a cause, activity, etc.

An engagement or obligation that restricts freedom of action.

Have you committed yourself to your spouse? We commit ourselves to so many things, so many people, but we often forget the ones that are closest to us. Think about the one thing or person that you loved as a child. Think back on how you cherished that thing or that person. Did you take care of it/them? Did you love it/them? Did you connect with it/them often?

Now it is time for you to show that same level of commitment to your husband and your marriage. Marriage is a daily walk, much like your walk with Christ. It takes daily renewing and fellowship. It required communication and honesty. The vows that you made to love him are in full effect. There will be many obstacles along the way. Some will be human nature and others will be planted by the enemy. I want you to know that the source of the obstacle is not the primary focus. The primary focus is getting past the obstacle and back into the core pf the relationship, which is love. The bible says that love covers a multitude of sin. (1 Peter 4:8, love is charity) Your commitment will be challenged. Sometimes we think that because we love each other the relationship will be perfect or that they would never do x, y, or z if they love me. While there is some truth to those statements, that does not mean that they do not love you. Often times we do not love ourselves when we commit acts against our marriage. The questions to ask yourself are:

- Do I love them enough to attempt to fix what is broken?

- Am I committed to them enough to trust the process of healing?

- Do I trust that God is amid this situation?

- Am I being led by my emotions or being directed by God?

Remember love is more than an emotion, it is a choice. There have been times in my marriage that my husband or I could have called it quits, but we were more committed to the call of God than to our individual feelings. We were not led by emotions, but we were led by God. We asked God in prayer to lead us. What we must realize is that our commitment to God is greater than any other commitment that we make. You made those vows in front of God and at least two witnesses, and God does not take that lightly. That is why you must seek Him first when there is a situation that goes against the marriage vows. He will release you if that is His Will and you will be at peace with it. (In cases of domestic violence know that God will not require you to stay there and suffer. Get help so that you can leave the situation please) Bottom line, activate your commitment by seeking God first and then obeying His commands.

Commitment goes both ways but just because your spouse decides to be disobedient to God and ignore their vows does not give you a "Hall Pass." Tit for Tat never works in relationships and vengeance will not make you feel better to correct the situation. Two wrongs never make the situation right. Do the right thing and you will be rewarded by God.

Healing

    the process of making or becoming sound or healthy again.

This is what this entire book hinges on, your ability to do that work that is needed to create a marriage that is healthy, whole and where God is the head of you both. This is a process, and it will never be perfect. This is a race not a marathon. The race is given to the ones that endure until the end. The definition gives the implication that there was a time when the marriage was wounded, but now in the healing process the marriage is becoming healthy again. I want you to know that we have all been at this place. We have all been wounded in some shape, form, or fashion. Now it is time to allow healing to take place. That means allowing time and space for you both to grow, mature, forgive, forget, renew, restore, and evolve.

We wound each other because we are broken, we are not mature, we are ignorant of facts. Some wounds are intentional, and others are unintentional. Some wounds are personal attacks while others are collateral damage. No matter the nature of the wound, you must believe that healing is possible, then you must accompany that belief with doing the work for change. Faith without work is dead. (James 2:17) So when you really believe that God has ordained your marriage to be successful now is the time to utilize the tools in this book to start your healing journey. This journey is not only for your marriage, but it is for you as an individual.

I can remember when I cried out to God to save my marriage. I initially thought God was just going to change my husband because I felt that he was the one who needed to change. But God changed my perspective really fast. He showed me how important my role as a wife was and how I needed to be dedicated to Him first if I wanted my marriage to be healed. He began to change my vision. I began to see my husband through the eyes of God. I realized that Good loved him too. I began to empathize with him. I saw the efforts that he was making as well as the issues that he was dealing with. I BEGAN TO PRAY FOR HIM. Ladies!!! Wives!! Women!!! This was the beginning of the transformation. When I began to pray God's Will over my husband's life things began to change for the good. His attitude changed. He began to listen to me, but most important, HE BEGAN TO LISTEN TO GOD and changed his behavior. Nothing happened overnight, but the changes were evident.

That is not to say that we did not or that you will not have setbacks. They will come but be of good cheer, you will overcome them. Most times that hardest step is the first one. When you are having a hard day or you are reminded of a past transgression, pray. Allow God to show you why you began the journey. I can say from experience that our journey was well worth it. I cried some days, wanted to fight some days, cursed some days, and even questioned God some days but if I had to, I would do it again. The husband and Man of God that I have today is a living testament of God's goodness, grace, and mercy. Put your war clothes on. IT'S TIME TO FIGHT!!! You are not fighting your spouse; you all are on the same team. It is the enemy who will be DEFEATED!!!

Healing: the process of making or becoming sound or healthy again.

> Psalm 147:7 He health the broken in heart and bindeth up their wounds.

Healing is a process. I worked as a Wound Nurse at one point in my career. It was a very tedious, sometimes smelly, job that required me to be quite meticulous. There was very little room for error. Errors in treating wounds can lead to more infection and deterioration of the skin. The skin is the largest organ of the human body, so when it is compromised, it can lead to other life-threatening situations. The healing process for a wound has to be strategically mapped out. The larger and more complex the wound, the greater the probability that the treatment will be unique to that patient. Some patients would refuse to let the nurse care for their wounds. When that happened, the wound got worse. It would get slimy, mussy, bigger and boy would it reek!! It would get to the point where they had to go to the hospital for treatment. Their blood would be infected, a term called septicemia. Now let's relate the healing process for the wound to the marriage.

There are many ways to be wounded within the marriage. Not to be a Negative Nancy but you need to be prepared for it before the problems arise. It is always better to be proactive rather than reactive. Back to the story, lol. Problems in your marriage are like infections, they can get large and seemingly out of control and they really stink!! When this happens, you need to be open to the healing process. When you decide to stay in the marriage yet refuse to allow the healing process to begin your marriage will be infected and eventually it will stink. Everyone will know that the marriage is going sour. So, what does allowing the healing process to begin mean?

First you must be open to healing. Maybe you told yourself prior to marriage that if your partner cheated on you that you would get a divorce immediately. Now you have been in this marriage for 5 years and infidelity has crept in. What do you do? What is your next move? You love him. He apologized, but you said that if this ever happened you would divorce immediately. Do you leave because of a vow you made before you were ever married or do you open your mind to the possibility that your marriage can be healed. Because you are reading this book lets go with option number 2. This is where you begin the healing process. These are the basics of the process no matter the issue:

1. Prayer. This is going to take daily prayer. Listen to God for direction.

2. Marriage Coaching and Therapy. This is the time to sort it all. You must be open to dealing with all the elephants in the room. This is not the time to be shy. This is the time to be totally honest. Remember that this is a PROCESS, and processes take time. The next steps will be support by your Coach/Therapist. If your spouse has not agreed to

go to therapy or has not committed to saving the marriage, then these sessions are for you and your personal healing. Healing begins with the individual and spreads aboard.

3. You and your spouse need to decide on the terms of your reconciliation.

4. Try to limit inquiring about the details of the affair and focus on the steps needed to heal your marriage specifically.

5. Personally, you must begin to work on you. Make sure that you are seeking God to heal your heart. Create boundaries, for yourself and for your spouse. You want to guard your heart while not allowing it to harden.

6. Continue to pray. Be very selective about who share your martial issues with, especially if you plan on staying in the marriage. Sharing with the wrong people can impede your healing process.

I have given you the steps to begin the process. How it ends it up to you and your spouse. The key is to heal is to have an open mind to the possibilities. Your desire to heal must be stronger than the pain that you are feeling. Yes, your heart is broken, trust may be lost, the pain seems to strong to go away, BUT you can and you will keep moving. You can keep moving broken or you can make the decision to keep moving and be whole. When you embrace the healing process you make the decision to become whole again.

Prayer:

Lord, right now in the name of Jesus I thank you for healing power. I thank you for giving me a mind to receive healing. I thank you because your Word says that by your stripes I am already healed. My marriage needs healing. My mind needs healing. My heart needs healing. Your Word says that you heal the broken hearted and you bind up their wounds, Lord, I need you right now to bind up my wounds in the mighty name of Jesus. I trust you Lord with my pain I trust you Lord with the trauma, I cast all my cares on you because I know that you care for me.

Your word commands me to pray for my enemies and those that despitefully misuse me. Now Lord I pray for my spouse. I pray that he seeks you first. I pray that you created him a clean heart and renew the right spirit within him. I pray that we can come together and heal our marriage. My desire is to keep my vowels, but Lord I ask that your will be done. I believe that you put us together and I rebuke the enemy and the part that he played in this situation. I surrender our marriage to You. Be with us as we go to counseling. Be with us as we navigate life and repair what has been broken, Give us grace for this journey. Order our steps in your Word, Draw us closer to you. Give us peace the surpasses our understanding. Allow our marriage to be a testament of Your goodness, Your Grace, and Your Mercy. In Jesus Name, Amen, and Thank God.

Heart Work

For where your treasure is, there will your heart be also. Matthew 6:21 KJV

Heart work when you say, "heart work", what comes to mind? Marriage and relationships are matter of the heart. They must encompass more than merely a fleshly desire for them to be successful. Love is a matter of the heart. Many times, it seems as though our heart has betrayed us. We think that we want one thing when we want another. Or is that we need one thing more than we desire than we desire the other thing. The Bible tells us not to trust our heart in some cases because it can be deceitful. (Jeremiah 17:9) That is why we must be led by the Holy Spirit. We ask God to cleanse our hearts and renew the right Spirit within us. (Psalm 51:10) This is a very personal process. This process taught me how to love God first and then love my husband through the eyes of God. I had to ask God to show me what he saw in my husband. Reveal what is good, what is pure, and what is of a good report. Open my spiritual eyes so that I see my husband as the man that you created him to be. When I began to see him as God saw him, my heart began to change. I became more forgiving. I was more open to communicate. I was able to look beyond his faults and see his needs.

I saw that he needed me to pray for him daily. I saw that he was fragile and that he was struggling with some weaknesses. I saw that he wanted to do what was right, but he had been in the pit for so long that he had lost sight of the palace (God's kingdom). I saw that he was capable and worthy of restoration. I began to love him unconditionally. I reminded him of who he was in Christ. I calmed his fears and created a space of peace for him to regain his focus. I made sure that when he came home that there was peace and quiet. The house was cleaned and the kids in order. I played gospel music to set the atmosphere. He saw me praising God even when he had given me reason to do otherwise. Absolutely nothing was able to steal my joy because I had cast all my cares on Jesus. I knew that this was a temporary store and that we would come out with a testimony. There were many hard days, and nights that we both cried but threw it all we both learned to focus on God and His redeeming power. Out trust for each other grew as did our trust in God. We began a daily devotional together. We would read a chapter of the book of Psalms each day and then we read the book of Proverbs. It was amazing. The Word of God drew us closer together. We were a three braided cord, God, Him and Me. We had all that we needed to BECOME whole again. Then God led us to our mentors, Mr. and Mrs. Vance. They coached us back to marital health. It was a process, but it was worth every moment. Our trials truly made us stronger. Yours will do the same if you follow God's instruction.

Acknowledgement

acceptance of the truth or existence of something:

the action of showing that one has noticed someone or something:

the action of expressing or displaying gratitude or appreciation for something:

We all want to be acknowledged. We all want to be accepted, especially by the people that we love. It is not unusual for us to expect acknowledgement from those that we love and that love us. Too many times we take each other for granted within our marriage. We make assumptions, ignore that issues, and keep silent all in an effort to "keep the peace." That is one of the worst things that we can do. I tell couples all of the time that they need to address the "elephant in the room." The hard topics are the ones that need to be addressed. You unpack the baggage in relationships by having conversations that allow for transformation.

Have you ever heard the adage; Actions speak louder than words? I believe that it is true. We say a lot of things, but it only matters when our actions back up our words, especially after a traumatic experience. Being a person of action is paramount in a marriage. Honoring your words is what develops trust and respect. When you are honest with your spouse in action and words, they realize that they can trust the words that you say, but when you say one thing and do another that lose that trust in your words. They lose their sense of security.

Maybe you are the one that has lost that trust. Maybe your spouse told you that he would love you and protect you and his actions have proven otherwise. How do you get past the trauma and regain trust? This is where action and acknowledgment come into play. Not only is there a need for there to be a change in the actions of the individual but there must be an acknowledgement of the wrong that has been done against the marriage, against the trust, against the respect. Many times, spouses feel like their needs. The hurt and pain has not been acknowledged. We want to know that you believe what I am not only saying but how I feel about what I am saying. This is also why I suggest therapy, coaching & counseling. These are areas within a marriage that require a moderator, a person outside of the relationship that can hear both of you and properly reflect on steps for reconciliation and healing.

When you do not get a change of actions or acknowledgment that means you must advocate for self-care and healing on a personal level. That means you get in a position to be healed regardless of how your spouse responds. This is personal. Go to therapy, join the women's group, get counsel from your Pastor, or hire a mentor. Either way get the help that you need to heal from every pain or trauma.

So today start acknowledging each area in your life. Acknowledge the issues, the victories, acknowledge who you are and what changes you desire to make. Take it day by day but keep moving. Come together with your partner and go over these items. Discuss how you both can support each other as well as support the marriage. Accept the truth of where and who you are today. Change the things that you do not like. Come to peace with the things that you cannot change. Allow the power of God to be activated in your marriage. What you feel that you cannot do, He can.

Necessary

Required to be done, achieved, or present; needed, essential.

It is necessary. Fantasia Barrino, singer, actress, and winner of 3rd season of American Idol has a song out titled, "Necessary". In that song she tells a story of how her hard times were necessary. Those times created character and helped her BECOME the woman that she is today. I want to encourage you. The rough times help create the person God ordained you to be. I know that we live in a time where people want a soft life, but I promise you if you endure these hard times, better days are on the way. Times of pruning, purging, and repositioning are necessary.

Diamonds, silver and even gold all must go through the refiner's fire. When a diamond is a clump of coal no one gives it a second look, but when it put under pressure and comes out as a sparkling, seemingly, flawless diamond its value goes up astronomically. You may be in a position where you are the lump of coal but when you allow God to get you through each test you will come out looking like that diamond. Your self-worth will increase, your relationship will grow, you will see life through the eyes of God. You will see your mate through the eyes of God. Things will not be perfect as the world views perfection, but you will be WHOLE.(whole is the Hebrew definition of perfection) So yes Sister, this is necessary, but it shall pass. During this process I suggest that you begin to journal. Write down your thoughts and prayers. Later you will be able to look back and see all the progress that you have made.

Nature or Nurture

The things in our life that are biologically motived versus the things that are taught.

Do you believe that you are prepared to be a wife? Do you believe that it is the nature of women to be wives? I believe that there is a very good possibility that you are wife material. The question is, "Do you want to nurture that calling?" The fact is that some things come naturally, and other things need to be nurtured into full maturity. So, if you do not feel that you naturally have what it takes to be a wife you are reading the right book. Even those that have a natural affinity to be wives can be taught. Consider yourself in class.

I am a believer in the idea that experience is not the best teacher in most cases. I am writing this book because I do not want you to have to experience every obstacle in marriage that I have endured. I would not have endured so much dysfunction of I had listened to those who had been married and to God. Take the lessons that you learned from watching those that have been married and use them to make your marriage better. Now I been around some bitter women that sat and gossiped about marriages and berated their husbands. I learned that I did not want to be the kind of wife. How is it that you talk bad about the man that you dedicated your life to? That says more to me about you and your decision making than it does about him. My advice to you is use the ideas and concepts that help build a healthy, whole marriage and the rest throw away. Allow God to lead you and guide you as to what is the best path for your marriage. God will never lead you into sin, so adultery & polygamy are out of the question. (humor) Our connection with God and the Holy Spirit is so important. For one couple infidelity may lead them to divorce court. For another couple it may lead then to counseling the allows them to restore what has been broken. God ordained marriage and he blesses those that handle marriage as He instructed in His Word.

Marriage is honorable and the bed undefiled. (Hebrew 13:4)

The concepts and ideas that you are in question about regarding your marriage are found in His Word. So, if you do not know or understand, search the scriptures. Then pray for revelation knowledge on how to proceed. Do not believe the tales of discontented women or women who have a cult like belief, marriage is neither contentious nor cult like. Being a wife is something that must be taught. None of us come into it as experts. Even if you have been married several times, you are not an expert in your current marriage. You have learned some things along the way but navigating life with each spouse is different. You need to be open to learn and be open to the voice of God. When me and my husband were experiencing hard times, I did not want to keep smiling, keep loving on him or even thinking good about him, but God told me to do all those things. The thing is that although you may not know all the ins and outs of marriage. God did indeed design you to be a wife. He created women as a helpmeet for man. Marriage is how we help our husbands, and together we create a family. When things are not coming together naturally. Feel free to contact God through his Word and prayer.

When our car is broken, we go to the user's manual and see what needs to be done. There are times when we can fix it ourselves and there are times when the car has to be sent to the shop. In other words, there are times when an issue can be fixed by simply changing our behavior or our words, and then there are times when we need outside assistance. Either way, God should be the first and most vital part of the equation. Ask God what the next move is. Pray and read His Word for guidance. This is a prayer that you can use to start the conversation. Remember the other intricate part about praying (talking) to God is LISTENING FOR HIS ANSWER.

Father God, I come to you in the name of Jesus. You are my creator and I trust You to lead me in every aspect of my life. I understand that You ordained marriage, and the marriage is honorable in your eyesight. (Genesis 2:18) Please reconstruct our marriage. Allow us to remember our vows and renew our love for each other. Allow my husband to love me like You love that church and allow me to respect and love him. Heal what is broken in each of us. Bind us closer together as your Word say that what you put together let no man take asunder. (Matthew19:6) Let our actions align with your Word.

Remind us to acknowledge each other, celebrate each other, and display our love for each other.

As a wife I acknowledge that I am my husband's help meet. I am here to help him thorough prayer and submission. As he submits to you, I submit to Him. I commit to being the help meet that you desire to me to be. In the name of Jesus. Amen and thank God.

Grace

God's favor

Favor – an act of kindness beyond what is due or usual.

God gives us new grace & mercy every day. We do not deserve it, but He gives it to use free of charge. We have not earned His grace. He gives it to us because He loves us. When we go through changes in our life, specifically in our marriage, we need grace. We also need to extend grace to others. As you are navigating this hard time in your marriage there will be days when you feel like giving up on your partner or giving up on the relationship. You may grow weary, tired, and overwhelmed. That is the time to extend yourself some grace, as well as some grace to your partner as you both have made a commitment to work things out.

In the world that we live in today we are not taught to extend grace. When someone has done us wrong, we are taught to throw them away. We are taught to discard anyone or anything that rubs us the wrong way. I want to remind you that marriage is more than a verbal commitment. Marriage is a covenant agreement between you, your spouse and God. It is the coming together of two souls with the Spirit of God covering you both, binding you both together. It is not to be taken lightly. Take this time to remember that love that you both shared on your wedding day. The joy of seeing all of your loved ones celebrate with you as you begin to start a life together. That same joy can be rekindled if you make the decision to extend grace.

You may be saying he does not deserve to be forgiven, he does not deserve my grace, I want to remind you that the very essence of grace is that it is not earned or deserved. God does not continue to show up for us because we have been so good or because we are so faithful. He shows up for us because He loves us, and He is true to His Word. (Romans 11:6 And if by grace, then it is no more of works: otherwise, grace is no more grace.) This is bigger than you and your husband. This is not only about God healing your marriage, but it is also about the enemy being defeated. The enemy has constructed a full-on attack on not just your marriage but on all marriages. If he can convince the world that marriages are not necessary, marriages do not work, that even "saved' folks are divorcing, then he will think that he has won. I want you to know that you are on assignment. Your assignment is to extend grace to your spouse, to declare & decree health and wholeness over your marriage, to do the work to change the trajectory of your marriage. Accept the call of God for restoration in marriage. Trust God to create the marriage that He desires for you and your spouse, one that is a testament of His goodness, GRACE, and mercy over your life.

My Grace is sufficient, signed God.

Grace is a gift from God that none of us truly deserve but he gives us new grace with each day. You will find that in marriage you both must give each other grace. Even when you do not think that your spouse deserves it, if you desire to restore your marriage you must extend grace. I have counseled women who were ready to throw in the towel. They had made up in their minds that the marriage was over. Then God spoke to their spirit and said, Be Still. (Psalms 46:10) Many times we are of the feel that our spouse does not love us if there is any discretion against the marriage. But think about it, does God not love us when we sin? He does not like the sin but he does not throw us away. He gives us chance after chance to restore our relationship with Him. Now I am not saying that you should allow your spouse to consistently sin against your marriage. What I am is that you should be obedient to the Will of God for your marriage and not be led by your emotions.

What I have found is that the enemy deals with our negative emotions. He wants us to be afraid, sad, angry, offended, mad, and unforgiving. He does not want is to be at peace, so he constantly feeds our mind with thoughts that are designed to kill, steal, and destroy. On the other hand, God wants us to think on things that are of a good report. (Philippians 4:8) that means that you are not to rehearse the issue repeatedly in your mind or with your words. Think on rehearse words of healing. Recite and journal about what you desire for your marriage.

This is a marathon, not a race. These ideas and concepts take time to develop and become a part of your marital arsenal of tools. This is especially true when lying, cheating, and addiction are the culprits. These are issues that not only you as a wife need grace when dealing with them, but your spouse needs grace to overcome them. We must envision our spouses through the eyes of Christ. No longer harping on the sin but seeing who God is transforming them into and where He is taking the marriage. Obstacles can be building block for your marriage of you listen and obey the voice of God. That is why I suggest Couples Coaching, no situation is the same. How God tells me to deal with my marriage/husband may be different than what He directs you specifically to do. Let's make some declarations.

1. I will listen to God concerning my marriage.
2. I will not be led by my emotions.
3. God has the final say on how my marriage will turn out.
4. I submit my desires and dreams for my marriage to God.
5. I will extend grace to myself.
6. I will extend the grace that God has given me to my husband.
7. I will see my husband through the eyes of Christ.

Reference Scriptures:
1. 2nd Corinthians 12:9
2. James 4:6
3. Numbers 6:24-26
4. Ecclesiastes 4:9
5. Proverbs 31:10-31

The last part of C.H.A.N.G.E. is EVOLUTION, we will discuss this in the next chapter. Get ready.

Chapter 7

The Evolution

Evolution

the gradual development of something, especially from a simple to a more complex form

Your marriage is ever evolving. It is not a simple process. The world tries to make it seem like a simple process as they give you reasons to create an exit plan. There is nowhere in the Bible where it states that life, marriage, children, or careers would be easy. The Bible states that there will be storms, trials, and tribulations. They key to going through these things is the God promise that He will be there with us and that in the end we will have victory. The fact is that marriage is going to have ups and downs because you have been obedient to God. People say things like," It wasn't like this when we were just dating." Or "He never cheated when we were living together." At that point the enemy had not implemented his full attack but when we decide to be obedient to God we are in direct opposition to the will of the enemy. It is at that point that he pulls out all the stops and makes your life/marriage miserable.

So, your marriage will go from simple to more complex. There will be changes that neither of you anticipated. There will be distractions and times when you wonder if it was worth it. I am not writing to you because I believe in the longevity of marriage. I believe that when we make God the head of our marriage it has lasting power. I am writing this to let you know that there are steps that you can take to ensure that your marriage becomes all that you desire it to be and that if YOU BOTH DESIRE IT, it can stand that test of time. That means that even when the one thing happens that you never thought would happen you look to God for the answer rather than the common consensus of those around you. There are marriages that did not last for 6 months because of financial woes and those that have lasted for 60 years in the wake of infidelity. It is all a choice. You must make your choice based on the will of God for your life.

When my husband and I were having difficulties, I asked God if we should separate or divorce. Not because I didn't love him but because I was tired of all the fighting. God told me that He wanted me to stay in the marriage. He promised me that if I put Him first, my life with my husband would change for the better. Guess what? Things have changed and I am glad that we stayed together, but it did not change that day or the next day. It was a progression that did not start directly after I spoke to God, it would be months before my husband, and I decided to get counsel and START the process of repairing our marriage. I want you to ask yourself and God some questions.

1. Did God put me & my spouse together?
2. Have I asked God if He desire me to stay in this marriage?
3. What has transpired that makes me want to separate/divorce?
4. Can these issues be fixed with prayer, coaching/counseling?
5. Have I discussed these issues with my husband?
6. What was his response?

7. What role have I played in the dysfunction of this relationship?

8. Do I want to do what it takes to repair the marriage?

9. What can I do differently?

These are questions that need answers. You can answer these alone, then with your spouse or along with a Coach/Counselor. This will help you as you start the process of deciding if the marriage is repairable.

Part of the evolution is being mature as you go through the process of deciding. It means waiting on God as he leads you. It requires maturity and emotional intelligence. Remember that this is the person that you made vows to love and cherish for better to for worse. Just because the worse showed up does not mean that you get a pass to view the vows are null and void. Do not assume that because your mate has violated the marriage vows that they do not love you. (We love God, but do we always obey His commands?) We all have moments where we make a bad decision. That one decision does not sum up their love for you. Most of the time it was not even about you. Remember that we fight not against flesh and blood but against spiritual darkness in high places. The enemy goes to and fro seeking whom he can devour. That is not to take the responsibility of wrongdoing away but know that it is often bigger than one decision. There are many things that play into the decisions that we make and sometimes it is generational rather than situational. That means that it may be a result of an issues that has been passed down through their bloodline. Other times it is a knee jerk reaction to a situation that may or may not have anything to do with you or the present state of the marriage. That is why seeking God is so important. No two situations are alike. You cannot compare your marriage to another, especially when you do not know that ins and outs of their situation. Bottom line is that there is no cookie cutter marriage and no cookie cutter answers. So, I encourage you to:

1. Put God first.
2. Always keep the lines of communication open.
3. Get marriage maintenance even when there are not issues.
4. Pray before the problems present themselves.
5. Be honest with yourself and your mate.
6. Do not be ashamed of admitting there is a problem.
7. Address the elephant in the room.
8. Remember tone matters.

9. Seek Godly advice.

Chapter 8
Let's talk About Sex

Sexual intercourse : sexual contact between individuals involving penetration, especially the Insertion of a man's erect penis into a woman's vagina, typically culminating in orgasm and the ejaculation of semen.

Intimacy: the state of being intimate, which is marked by the consensual sharing of deeply personal information. It has cognitive, affective, and behavioral components. Intimates reveal themselves to one another, are comfortable in close proximity.

Sex is a major component in a marriage. It is usually the first thing that couples stop doing when there is trouble. This is a bad move to make. When sex is disrupted in a marriage that gives the enemy the opening that he needs to wreak even more havoc. Along with the disruption of sex comes the halting of intimacy. The couple is no longer cuddling, having pillow talk and all of the seemingly little things that bind the relationship together. This results in the couple looking to replace sex and intimacy by seeking another person who will provide it for them. This may be for what they intend to be a temporary basis, but it has an everlasting effect on the marriage. That is why it is so important to keep the "fire" lit in your bedroom even when there is a storm brewing.

So, what do you do when the sex and the intimacy are lacking or gone all together?

This is the time to have the "hard" conversations, get the help of a coach, counselor, or therapist. Discuss what the source of the disconnect is. Get to the root of the problem. The longer you go without coming together the more time the enemy has to work with. It put you and your marriage in a position for infidelity to occur. Cheating, emotional or physical, hurts all parties involved. This is not what you want, especially if you know that there is hope for your marriage. Now, I will be transparent. My marriage did suffer from infidelity and by the grace of Gid we made it past it. It was a long hard path that caused many tears, fears, and many apologies, I would not wish it on my wors t enemy. So. If you can, avoid it at all costs.

This is also a time of intense prayer. If your spouse is withholding sex, then you need to pray that God keeps him from seeking out anyone else and that the enemy does not present him with a willing participant. If you are the one who is withholding sex, you need to ask God to release whatever is making you not desire your spouse. I remember very early in my marriage I would withhold sex when the bills weren't paid or if we had had an argument. It was my way of punishing him for not handling things in the way that I thought that he should be handling them. This Not the right way to handle disagreements, and you should never be seeking revenge in your marriage. Remember you two are on the same team.

The bible speaks against keeping sex from each other. 1st Corinthians 7:2-5 says.

Nevertheless, to avoid fornication, let every man have his own wife, and let every woman have her own husband. 3 Let the husband render unto the wife due benevolence: and likewise, the wife unto the husband. 4 The wife has not power of her own body, but the husband: and likewise, the husband hath no power over his own body: but the wife. 5 Defraud ye not one another except it be with consent for a time, that ye may be give yourselves to fasting and prayer, and come together again, that Satan tempt not ye for your inconsistency.

That says it all in a nutshell. God knows that sexual intercourse and intimacy are vital components to marriage, and he gave us as couples free reign in the bedroom with one another. Hebrews 13:4: Let marriage be held in honor among all, and let the marriage bed be undefiled, for God will judge the sexually immoral and adulterous. God also states that there will be judgement on the immoral and adulterous. Sexual immorality changes the dynamics of a marriage. It brings people outside of the marital covenant into the marital bedroom. It breeds fear, anger, resentment, loneliness, regret, low self-esteem, contention , and many other emotions that push a couple further away from each other.

It is too late.

Is that how you feel? Has emotional or physical adultery already reared its ugly head into your marriage. I want you to know that even though lines have been crossed you can still save your marriage. Now, biblically adultery is grounds for divorce but that does not have to be your testimony. There need to be some new boundaries set for your marriage to be restored. The affair must come to a halt immediately. True recovery cannot occur until the affair is confessed by the spouse who carried on the affair. All ties with the outside party must be severed immediately. This is the time for the adulterer (for the lack of a better word) to come clean. This does not mean a play by play of each intimate detail or sexual escapade (believe me that will hurt you even more). I mean that this is the time to declare that they are willing to do anything within biblical principles and reasonable expectations to repair the marriage. It can be anything from changing jobs to changing residency. Actions are the first step in proving that you want the marriage, so if you need to or they need to change their cellphone number, change their route to school or change their place of worship, JUST DO IT.

    There will be days ahead when the marriage will be tested. You will not trust where he is going. You will probably want to always keep their location on. This is normal after trust has been broken but remember you cannot stay here forever. As you are shown that they are sincere in their motives and they really do love you, allow your heart to heal. Begin to date again, schedule time for fun and intimacy. Ask God to help you during this time of healing. Ask Hin to keep you aware of any red flags while healing your heart to receive true love from your spouse. The enemy comes to kill, steal and destroy bit God came that we may have life and have that life more abundantly. You are now on the journey to a new, better life with your spouse. Forgive and allow God to help you forget. None of this is over night but it is possible through Christ.

    1.Philippians 4:13 - "I can do all things through Christ which strengthened me."

2. Mark 10:27 - "And Jesus looking upon them saith, with men it is impossible, but not with God: for with God all things are possible."

3. Mark 9:23 And Jesus said to him, "'If You can?' All things are possible to him who believes."

It may seem impossible at this very present moment, but God is able to heal you from the inside out. Even if you both decide to end this marriage God will prepare you for your future husband. You will be healthy and whole.

There are so many issues that come along with infidelity that I cannot possibly deal with them all in this one chapter. I encourage you to seek wise counsel. Be honest with yourself about your feelings and allow them to be open and honest about their reasoning for the affair. Most importantly allow yourself that time to heal. Take baby steps if you must but keep moving in the right direction. Do not isolate yourself or feel guilt or shame. Keep God first in your life and allow Him to order your steps. Allow the Holy Spirit to be your comforter. This too shall pass.

Prayer:

Lord, in the name of Jesus,

Please fix what is broken in my marriage. There has been a breach of trust and infidelity. I love my husband and I am dedicated to repairing my marriage. I ask that you give me the strength to look beyond each indiscretion and see my husband for who You designed Him to be. If it is your will that we repair this marriage give me the strategy. Give me the heart to forgive and forget. Your Word says that a righteous man falls 7 times but can get back up. I know that my husband loves me. Please create in me and my husband a clean heart and renew the right Spirit within us both. I ask that you take the desire to be with any other women or commit any other sexual sin against our marriage. Mold him and make him into the man of God that you have purposed him to be. Allow us to get wise consult. Allow there to be no residuals of hate, shame, or guilt. I cover our marriage in prayer and the Blood of Jesus, in Jesus' name, Amen.

Scripture:

1. 2 Corinthians 5:17: "Therefore if anyone is in Christ, he is a new creature; the old things passed away; behold, new things have come."

2. Ephesians 1:7: "In him we have redemption through his blood, the forgiveness of our trespasses, according to the riches of his grace."

3. Mark 11:24: Therefore, I say unto you, What things so ever you desire, when ye pray, believe that ye receive them , and ye shall have them.

Bedroom Behavior

I am not a sex therapist, but I have been having sex, (good sex), for quite a while with my husband, over 25 years to be exact. I may just know a little bit about the subject. This portion of this book is for all the shy women, all the super Holy women who have not been open to allowing their husbands to make love to them. Take notes Sis. !!!

As stated earlier, the marital bed is undefiled. That means that the bedroom is pure for you and your husband. There are boundaries. There are not to be any other people or animals having sex with you and your husband, and the things that you both agree to do must be consensual by both of you. Be open and honest about your desires in the bedroom, no need to be shy. You have a lifetime to explore each other's bodies. Have fun. Do not let the opinions of others hold you two back. There is more than one enjoyable position. Missionary is not the only way to enjoy yourself. Be adventurous. Maybe you need or desire a toy or two, you will not go to hell. Remember that this is a time for you both to enjoy each other. Allow your hands, your mouth, your eyes to explore and find spots of ecstasy. God made the man for the woman and the woman for the man. There is an anointing on the marital bed, especially for those who waited until marriage to indulge in sexual pleasures. (Read Song of Solomon, I suggest the Tony Evans bible Translation, it will blow your mind).

So maybe you are saying. "I am not a virgin and I have expectations that my spouse is not meeting." I totally get it. Some people have had some wonderful experiences in the bedroom prior to marrying their spouse. There are soul ties and memories that may be attached to your sexual experiences. That is why it is so important to be prayerful. Open and honest. I want to be frank; Joey may have been dealing with 9 inches and your husband has 6 inches, now you think that the marriage is doomed. I want you to know that that does not have to be the case. You can teach each other what feels good and what is pleasing. You may both have to comprise in initially but with practice and maybe sex therapy you can find pleasure with your mate. Please do not be so easy to give up. Try new things, new positions. Talk to him, place his hand in the right spot. You both have to be open to getting to know each other. Sex is one of the areas that the enemy really wants to make difficult in a marriage. He wants any excuse to break down the marriage and separate those that love each other. It is the small foxes (issues) that destroy the vine (the marriage). Do not let the enemy win.

Prayer:

Lord, I am coming to you interceding for me and my husband. Your Word says that the marital bed is undefiled, and the sex was designed for the husband and the wife. My husband and I are not seeing eye to eye concerning our bedroom behavior. There are some issues from the past or things that have been taught that are hindering me from experiencing pleasure when we have sex.

I desire to enjoy my husband in every way. I ask that you allow us to enjoy ourselves. Open our eyes and ears to each other's needs. Destroy any stronghold or barrier to our sexual pleasure with one another. Destroy any soul ties and memory of sexual intercourse with anyone else. Lord, we thank you for freedom and purification in our bedroom. In Jesus name, Amen

Scriptures:

1. Genesis 1: 27-28

2. Genesis 2: 23-24

Nyenye – Rooted & Grounded

3. 1 Corinthians 7:1-8

4. 1 Corinthians 6:9

Notes:

Chapter 9

In-Laws, Stepchildren, Pets, Work Spouses and MORE

Let all things be done decently and in order. 1st Corinthians 14:40

I almost left this chapter out because most of this is simple common sense in my opinion. Then I remembered that my aunt Wavie told me many years that common sense is not common. It is not a flower the blooms in every garden. Lord, rest her soul. So here we are, I am including these things that are a part of many marriages but are mishandled in so many cases.

The bible tells the man to leave his mother and father and cleave to his wife. This means that the women, his wife becomes his priority. He leads her as God leads him, they create a family. Now that does not mean that the mother-in-law, father-in- law, siblings and other extended family members are thrown to the curb. They just have a different level of priority at this point. You two are a team and teams work together for what is best for the team as a whole. I have seen so many husbands who continue to cater to the needs of their mother while ignoring the needs of their wife and children. That should not be. The in-laws need to understand that the dynamics of their son's life has changed. They can and will be included in his life but not to the demise of his marriage.

There is a new term that I have been hearing lately called "emotional incest". It is where the mother of the son (or the father of the daughter) is so attached to their child that they behave as if they are romantically attracted to their child. This is a spirit from the enemy in my opinion. The connection between mother and sons or daughters and fathers need to be healthy and whole. They should not be filled with manipulation and deceit. The parent should not be jealous or envious of the new wife. This can be avoided by some simple conversations and by your husband being open and honest about the situation with you and his mother. There needs to be boundaries set that you both agree to adhere to. The mother is then given these guidelines. If she adheres to them the issues should gradually cease. It will take time for her to get on board, so please give some grace.

Boundaries are a part of life. We all need limits (boundaries) Matter of fact God even has them. Too many times these boundaries are ignored and our marriages, our lives become a breeding ground for chaos and confusion. That does not have to be your testimony. Many times, there are red flags that alert you to this type of behavior and you ignore it. Do not ignore red flags. So how do you deal with the stepchildren, pets, ex-girlfriends, nosey cousins, etc. Create ground rules in the very beginning. Once you are aware that the relationship is moving towards marriage these conversations need to be had. There should be boundaries that help create the relationship that you desire and strengthen the marriage. Remember the marriage relationship is the most important and then all other relationships stem from it. Respect must be a part of each relationship. The needs and desires of each person in the marriage need to be considered. Let me give some example scenarios.

Dealing with the Baby Momma/Ex- wife

This can be a nightmare or a walk in the park, you both get to decide. You and your husband must stand in agreement for the rules of engagement. There need to be scheduled times for the child(ren) to visit or spend the night, go on vacation, how they address the stepparent, etc. These need to be rules that you both are comfortable with and they are beneficial for the child. None of these rules should be based on revenge, hostility, or ill will towards the child or the baby momma/ex-wife. Be open, honest, and reasonable. Think about how you would feel in this situation. How would you want your spouse to respond. How would you want them to treat your child? How would you want the child to treat them?

There are so many aspects to these relationships and the key is to treat them the way that you would want to be treated if the situation were reversed. Extend grace when needed. Pray. Pray. Pray, God is a rewarder of those who diligently seek Him. Also remember that NOTHING IS IMPOSSIBLE FOR GOD.

Work Wives/Husbands

Now you might not like this, but this should not be. There is nothing wrong with having or being friends with your colleagues at work. But they should only have the title of friend. Our words are LIFE. Life and death are in the power of the tongue. We have what we say. So, when a person is given the title that should only belong to their spouse there is a problem. The enemy sees and hears this, and he begins to work. He creates inappropriate situations, feelings, and conversations. It becomes more than friendship and may even become an entanglement. We are spiritual beings and when we "open up" our hearts to people, we must be aware of how we are allowing them to pour into us. We must be led by the Spirit of God and not our flesh or emotions.

Emotional affairs are real. They can be just as damaging as physical affairs. When you begin to share things with a colleague that you do not feel comfortable sharing with your spouse, that is a red flag. When you look forward to getting to work so that you can be near that colleague, red flag. When you start belittling your spouse to that colleague, red flag. A real friend would notice this kind of behavior and bag off. But because they have been given the title of work spouse, they begin to meet your emotional needs. They begin to be the person that you desire, so much so that you no longer seek emotional support from your spouse. In some instances, the spouse becomes a nuisance, you simply do not want to be bothered. This is a real problem.

If you see this happening in your marriage there needs to be some immediate boundaries, put in place. There needs to be a conversation. There needs to be some marriage counseling /coaching. There needs to be prayer. You can get past this if you confront it. Ignoring the issue will only create bigger issues. The buck stops here. If your spouse denies that there is a problem, you PRAY. Ask God to separate them and to draw you and your spouse closer together. Speak the Word only. Marriage is between, God , You and Your Spouse, there is no room for work husbands/wives. Be clear about this early on. Anyone who seeks to meet the needs of your spouse or you, emotionally or physically, is a threat to the marriage. This includes exe's, best friends, mothers, baby mommas, cousins, etc. You both are one team. You do not need any extra players or fill-ins.

Prayer:

Lord,

I come to you asking you to retore my marriage. I ask you to allow us to be of one mind, and one spirit. I ask you to renew our minds in your Word. Allow us to see our marriage as the union between us and YOU. There are many things, issues, and people who have come against our marriage. My prayer is that these weapons will not prosper. Lord draw us closer together so that we see the needs of each other as important. Allow the love that we have for each other to cover a multitude of sins. Allows our minds to be renewed in Your Word. Purge and prune anything that is not like you. Allow us to be on one accord.

In Jesus name, Amen.

Note from the Author

I am excited for you!!! Thank You for trusting me and trusting the knowledge that God has imparted in me and I have written for you. My prayer is that it helps you and renews your hope for a healthy and whole marriage. I am available to Coaching and I have a Online Membership that can assist you with Marriage, Empowerment, and Relationships. Feel free to contact me via email at info@coachnyenyej.com .

Thank You Again & God Bless You

Acknowledgments

I will be forever grateful…

I want to thank God who gave me the grace and the wisdom to complete this book. I want to thank my family who have been so patient and kind, as I started and stopped so many times. Thank you all for believing in me when I did not believe in myself.

Special dedication to my father, Milton Caldwell, Jr. You inspired me to be all that I could be. You stressed education and excellence. You loved me and nurtured me. Even when times got bad, I knew that you loved me. Because of YOU, I am. Rest Up, Poparoni

To my mother, Brenda Caldwell… What can I say? You are a woman after God's own heart. You introduced me to Christ, The greatest gift of all. You showed me how to be a woman and a woman of God. You showed me what real dedication looks like in marriage and in life. God must really favor me because He gave me you as a Mom. I will forever be grateful. Because of YOU, I am. Love you, Brenda Sue.

Nyenye – Rooted & Grounded

To my Sister/Cousin, Dr. Taessa Malone-Carter, I LOVE YOU. You are a testament that hard work pays off. You have been through many trials and tribulations, but you always come out shining. You are an awesome woman of God, Sister, and Friend. I will always cherish you and our relationship. Thank You for never giving up on me and being my protector. I did it AFRAID!! Love you, Sis.

To my extended family, aunts, uncles, cousins, etc. There are too many of you to thank individually but I want you each to know that you hold a special place in my heart. I am so glad the I am a part of the Caldwell, Midgett, Jordan and Bunn families!!! You all are some of the kindest, loving, awesome people in the whole wide world!! Glad to call you FAMILY!!!

To my WWIC family, especially our fearless leader, Evangelist Jessica Williams, thank you for being a friend. Thank you for each prayer. Thank you for pushing me to finish the work that God had begun in me. Thank you for Blue Ridge, GA, where healing and deliverance took place. My life will never be the same. Love you guys to life!!!

To my children, my nieces, and nephews... ANYTHING IS POSSIBLE!!! Keep God 1st and allow Him to use you!! I love you and I keep you in my prayers. Continue to dream dreams knowing that with work and determination You will be Victorious!!! Love You All!!

Special Thanks to Tammy Jurnett- Lewis , Dr. Sheniqua Johnson, and Tamara Gooch, my forever SisterFriends!!! Thanks for being there for me, answering questions, calming my fears, and getting in my butt when necessary!!! I will always love you all!!!

Tammy – You started this. You pushed me to believe in me and my God given ability. I don't know how I will ever repay you.

Dr. Sheniqua – the marathon continues Sis!!! God is preparing a table just for YOU, I will always be your cheerleader!!

Tamara – You saw something in me that I did not see. I pray that journey of Sisterhood and Collaboration never ends.

To My Husband
Minister Auntwuan Jordan (My Pastor)
My Love, My Friend, My Confidante, My Buddy, My Co-Laborer in the Gospel

I love you. I want to thank you for allowing God to transform our marriage. I thank you for breaking the general curses of your life. I want to thank you for being patient and kind when I was mean and hateful. Thank you for being my friend. Thank you for not giving up or giving out. Thank you for being willing to separate yourself so that our marriage would thrive. Thank you for being obedient to God. Thank you for every sacrifice. Thank you for being a real man (thoroughbred), lol. I am so glad God sent me to you. Thank You for praying for me even before you understood the ramifications of marriage. Thank you for being the best father in the whole wide world Craig!!!! I would not want to do this life with anyone else but you. You are my ROCK, ROCK, ROCK, ROCK, ROCK (inside).

Two young kids created a life together. It has been the journey of my life, and the amazing part is it is nowhere near over. We have only just begun!!! So here is to another 25 plus years living , loving, and learning together. Love you Always & Forever. #AAMJFORLIFE

About the Author

Nyenye Jordan has co-authored three anthologies. She currently lives in Tennessee, but she was born and raised in Detroit, Michigan. She is the founder of Yahweh Daughter's Christian Fellowship. She is the CEO of Making Our Relationships Extraordinary (M.O.R.E.) and Cofounder of Neighboring Nurses Association, LLC. She is a dedicated Speaker, Author, Evangelist, Marriage & Empowerment Coach. Her life's purpose is to use her gifts to restore marriages and lead people to Christ.

Look out for more Christian Self-help guides for women and Christian Fiction novels. Nyenye is excited to connect with her supporters.

Connect with Nyenye

To connect with Nyenye, you can find her on:

Facebook – Nyenye Jordan

Instagram - @morewithnyenyej

Website – https://coachnyenyej.com/relationships

YouTube https://www.youtube.com/@CoachNyenyeJ

Email – info@coachnyenyej.com

Nyenye – Rooted & Grounded

Made in the USA
Columbia, SC
24 May 2024